What Archaeology Tells Us About Prehistory

by Ellen B. Cutler

Editorial Offices: Glenview, Illinois • Parsippany, New Jersey • New York, New York

Sales Offices: Needham, Massachusetts • Duluth, Georgia • Glenview, Illinois
Coppell, Texas • Sacramento, California • Mesa, Arizona

From History to Prehistory

History starts us on a journey back through time. History is about the rise and fall of kingdoms, advances in science and art, and religious beliefs. History is learned about through written documents. Any document—a government decree, a shopkeeper's accounts, or a young person's journal—can provide facts and information about a **culture**.

Cultures existed long before the invention of writing, however. The period before the invention of writing is known as **prehistory**. History is about five thousand years old, but prehistory is much, much older.

The story of the past is told through both words and objects.

Archaeologists at a dig work slowly and carefully on the artifacts that they find.

Connecting Artifacts to Cultures

Artifacts are the main source of information about prehistory. **Archaeologists** search for artifacts, identify them, and determine their age. Anthropologists, or people who study **anthropology**, use these objects to try to understand the lives prehistoric peoples led.

Archaeologists looking for artifacts set up an excavation site, or dig. Before they begin digging, however, they make a map of the area and divide it into small sections called units. The units help show exactly where each artifact is found—how deep in the ground it is and how near it is to shelters, fireplaces, or other living areas.

The earth is made up of layers of dirt, stone, and other material, and each layer is connected to a particular period of time. An artifact is likely to be the same age as the layer of earth in which it was found.

While some dirt can be removed with shovels or machines, most of it is cleared away with brushes and tiny tools that will not break or scratch delicate artifacts. Some of the dirt is set aside in buckets. Later on, the dirt is sifted through a screen that separates out broken stone tools or pieces of bone.

Culture Versus Civilization

Is there a difference between culture and civilization? There is a difference to an anthropologist. A **civilization** is an advanced culture with different social levels. Civilizations are connected to city life. In fact, the word *civilization* comes from the Latin word *civis*, meaning "citizen," or a person living in a city or town. One might say that all civilizations are cultures, but only some cultures can be called civilizations.

How old is really old?

Another way to determine the age of an artifact is by **carbon dating**. All living things—plants and animals—contain several forms of the element carbon, including carbon 14 (C14). As soon as a plant or animal dies, C14 starts to disappear. It takes about fifty thousand years to disappear completely. Carbon dating can accurately date many types of plants and animals that are not older than fifty thousand years.

Paintings, too, can be carbon dated. If a cave painting, for instance, has black paint made from burnt wood or bone, a scientist can determine the amount of C14 in the paint. This is how archaeologists determine the age of a cave painting.

Dating Prehistory

Determining when prehistory began is more difficult than deciding when it ended. While most scholars agree that prehistory began with human culture, there is considerable argument as to when humans developed culture.

Some say that prehistory goes back to the appearance of our earliest ancestors. Others say prehistory started about 2 million years ago when early humans began to use tools. Still others date the start of prehistory to 100,000 years ago and the development of the first modern humans.

Defining Culture

In anthropology the word *culture* refers to the shared experience of a group of people. These experiences are beliefs and learned knowledge.

Social attitudes are beliefs. Such beliefs might cause a person to give special consideration to some members of a family or treat one group differently than another group.

Learned knowledge might include the best place to catch fish or which plants are good to eat. Using fire, designing tools, and caring for people who are sick or injured are other forms of knowledge. In a culture, knowledge is not only handed down from one generation to the next. It is constantly improved.

Some prehistoric cities had stone buildings and large temples.

Where do the words come from?

Many of the technical words used by archaeologists come from the Greek language.

The earliest, or oldest, part of the Stone Age is called the Paleolithic period. The prefix *paleo-* comes from *palaio,* which means "ancient" or "long ago." The suffix *-lithic* comes from the Greek word for stone. The Neolithic era is the most recent part of the Stone Age. The prefix *neo-* comes from *neos,* which means "new."

Prehistory and the Age of Stone

Prehistory is divided into three ages based on the **technology** used. These ages are the Stone Age, the Bronze Age, and the Iron Age. Although scientists disagree as to when each of these ages ended and the next began, it is clear that our prehistory took place almost entirely in the Stone Age.

During the Stone Age humans made tools and personal objects from stone, wood, bones, and shells. Toward the end of the Stone Age, people built permanent settlements. **Agriculture** became the center of life, and people planted grains and other plants. They domesticated, or tamed, animals, such as cows, horses, goats, and dogs.

More skill and better materials led to better tools.

Small Clovis point

Folsom point

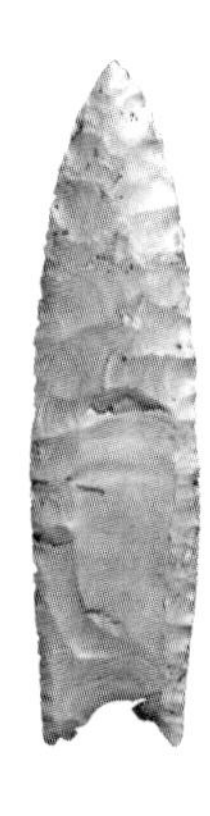

Larger Clovis point

Slated spear point

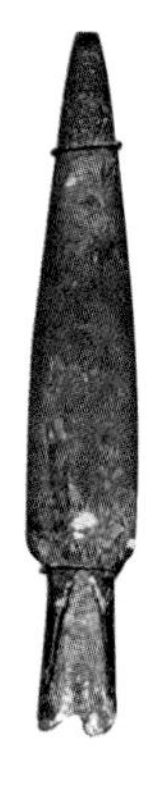

Copper spear point

Chipped-stone spear point

A bronze axe is an example of an early tool.

The Ages of Metal

Late Stone Age peoples learned to heat copper ore to get copper, a soft metal that breaks easily. Bronze is a hard and useful alloy made by mixing molten copper and tin. An alloy is a mixture made by melting different metals together.

The Iron Age began at the end of the Bronze Age, about 3,000 years ago. Iron is more difficult to work with than bronze, but it is stronger. Iron tools were much better than those made of copper and bronze.

In some places around the world, the Stone Age was followed directly by the Iron Age. Some Stone Age cultures survived so long, however, that contact with technologically advanced civilizations launched them directly into the modern world. In general, however, the invention of written language, whatever a culture's technology, signaled the end of prehistory.

Writing appeared in Egypt and in what is now Iraq about five thousand years ago. Ancient China had a system of writing about four thousand years ago. The Aztecs, who lived in Mexico seven hundred years ago, never developed a written language, although they did use a system of simple pictures to keep records.

Time Line of Prehistory

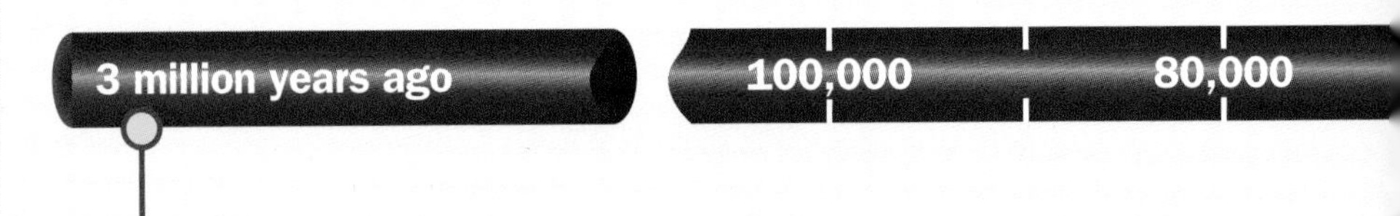

The break in the time line means that a part of the time line has been left out. In this case the years between 3 million years ago and 100,000 years ago have been left out of the time line.

Finding, growing, and preparing food are all forms of knowledge.

Progress During the Stone Age

The Stone Age lasted about 2.5 million years. During this time, humans developed and spread from the African continent throughout Europe, Asia, and North and South America.

By the end of the Stone Age, **nomads**, who moved from place to place in search of food, had become farmers who lived in villages. Small family groups became larger societies in which people took on different roles.

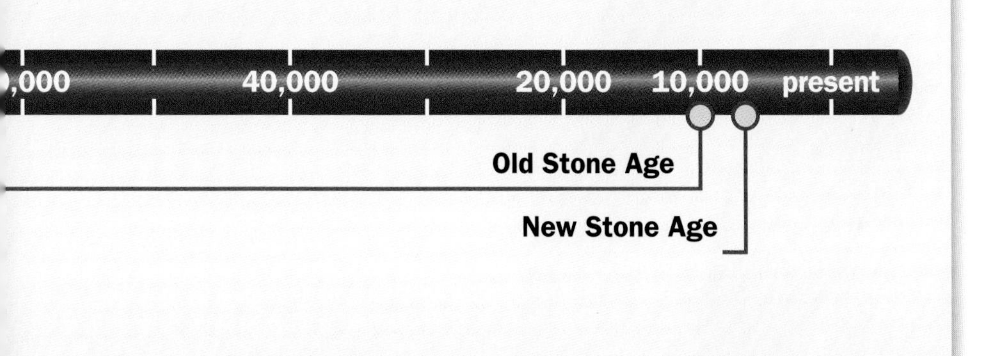

Mastering Fire

Perhaps the most important "tool" in prehistory was fire. Our ancestors were warming themselves with fire about 450,000 years ago.

At first, early humans may have taken advantage of small fires caused by lightning. They later figured out how to control these fires and keep them burning. Finally they discovered ways to create fire themselves.

Fire served humans in many ways: it kept them warm in cold weather and protected them from wild animals. Cooking made foods taste better, and meat dried in smoke did not spoil. A crackling fire would have encouraged people to gather together for warmth, safety, and social reasons. Small fires made it possible to work at night and in dark caves.

Fire was important to prehistoric cultures.

This flint-bladed dagger and a woven-grass pouch were probably used around the New Stone Age.

The First Tools

The first tools—axes, scrapers, and knives—were made from rocks that had been broken to produce a sharp edge. Later Stone Age peoples learned to flake thin pieces from large rocks. These flakes had sharp edges and points. Attached to sticks or long bones, the flakes became arrows and spears or scythes for cutting grasses and grains.

Stone was not the only material used to make tools. A variety of points, including spearheads, awls for poking holes in skins, and sewing needles, were made from bone, antler, and ivory.

Prehistoric Music

Musical instruments are among the most ancient artifacts. Hollow bones, especially the bones of birds, were perfect for use as flutes. All they needed were finger holes cut or bored into the bone so that the flute player could make different sounds. Stone Age cultures also made rattles and drums.

Carved Objects and Personal Ornaments

The oldest prehistoric pieces of artwork were small, portable carvings, such as animal and human figures. Personal ornaments made from ivory, shells, and animal teeth were also common. Some hunters decorated their weapons. This is the kind of art one might expect in a nomadic culture.

Did these works of art have a purpose or a special meaning? For instance, were ivory beads valuable? Did a shell necklace show that the owner was an important person? Perhaps an animal figure served as a good-luck charm. There is no way to know for certain.

In addition to paintings, prehistoric people made fine rock carvings, such as this scene that was discovered near Les Eyzies, France.

Paintings and Wall Decorations

The most remarkable works of prehistoric art may be the paintings filling caves that extend far underground. To make paint, artists ground colored substances into powder and mixed the powder with water or animal fat. Minerals dug from the ground produced yellow, brown, and red colors. Black came from burnt bones and wood. The artists dabbed the paint onto stone with their fingers or with twigs, or used brushes made from animal hair. They also blew powdered color through hollow bones.

Animals were the most common subjects of cave paintings and included wild cattle, horses, deer, lions, woolly mammoths, rhinoceros,

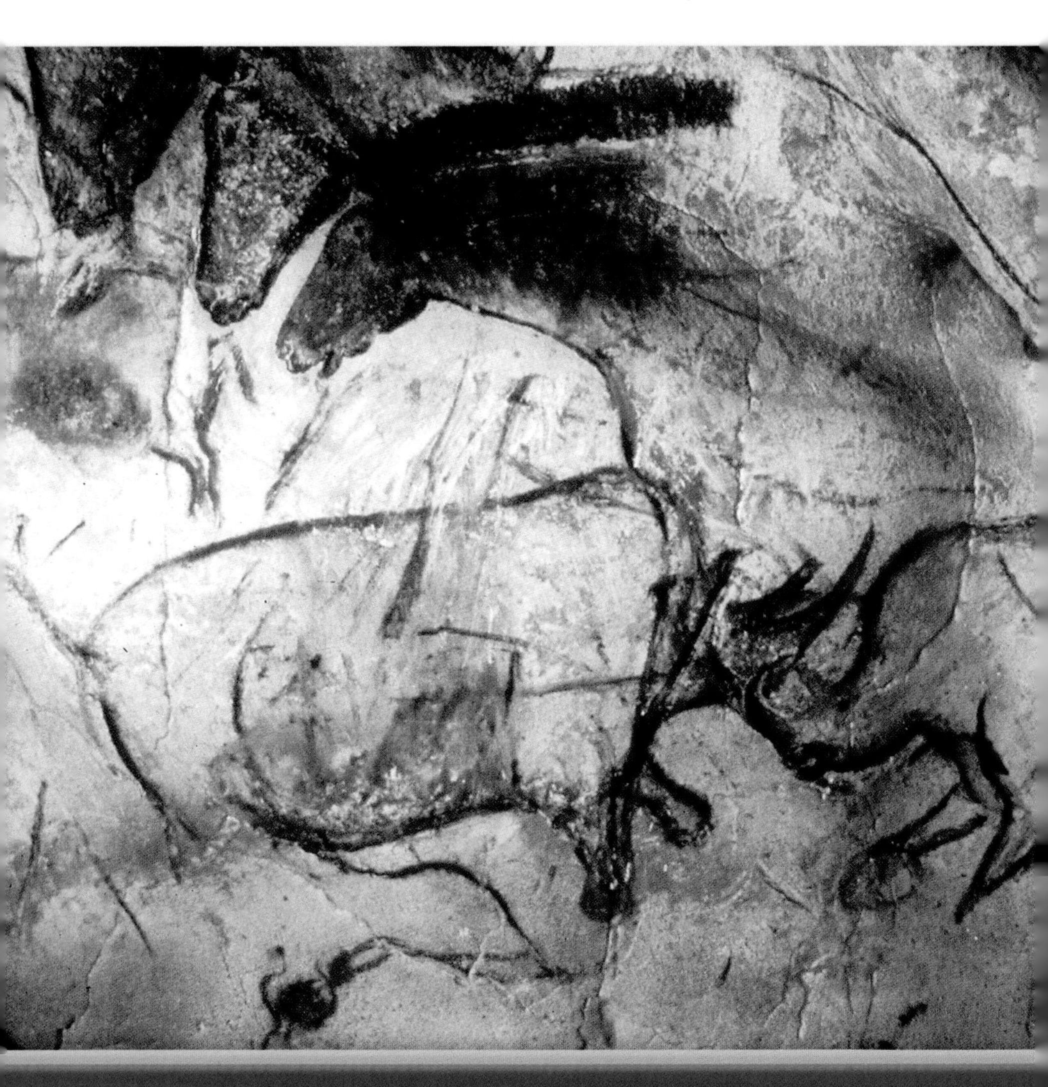

and goats. Human figures show up from time to time, but the outlines and prints of human hands are more common. Dots, zig-zags, and spirals also frequently occur in surviving cave paintings.

As with the small carvings, the purpose and meaning of these paintings are a mystery. The caves were not used as homes. They are dark, damp, and remote. The pictures themselves were often placed high on the walls and can be hard to see.

One theory suggests that the paintings were intended to bring the hunters luck. Many cave paintings show horses, wild cattle, and deer. Prehistoric people hunted all of these animals in great numbers. Other animals that appear in the paintings, such as the rhinoceros, however, were not usually hunted for food. The cave paintings at Chauvet in southern France show at least two separate images of rhinoceros fighting with each other. It is possible that prehistoric people admired the great strength of the rhinoceros and painted them for that reason.

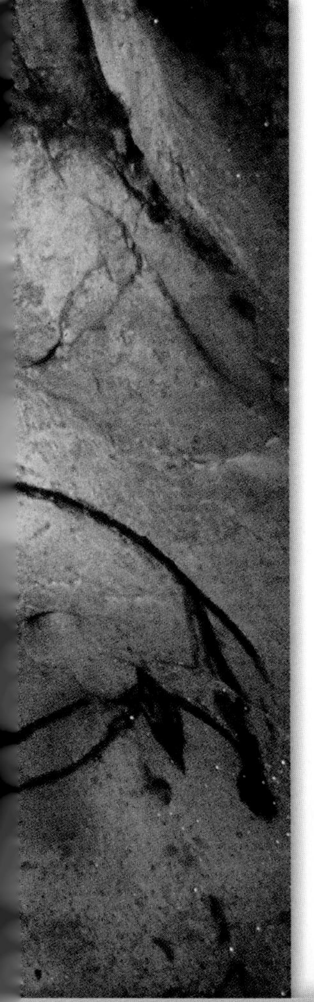

This cave painting in Chauvet, France, depicts images of horses and rhinoceros.

Other theories suggest that some animals represented spirits or forces that Stone Age peoples feared or worshipped. Perhaps the caves were used for religious ceremonies.

Some scholars share the theory that the cave paintings were records of important ideas and events. Such pictures might have been used to keep memories alive. From this point of view, cave paintings are historical documents similar to written records.

This cave painting of a man and a bison was discovered by teenagers in Lascaux, France.

"New" Paintings: The Chauvet Cave

Some "new" cave paintings have turned out to be some of the oldest. In 1994 a group of three friends explored some caves in southeastern France. They found an area inside one cave that seemed blocked by a pile of dirt and rocks. They dug through this barrier and explored the cave. It was dark and the only light came from their flashlights.

To their astonishment they saw woolly a mammoth outlined in red on a rock hanging from the ceiling of the cave. The more they looked, the more pictures they found—horses, rhinoceros, bulls, lions, human handprints, and patterns of dots—on almost every surface. The artist or artists had recorded creatures that roamed the earth more than 32,000 years ago.

The cave now belongs to the French government. It was named for Jean-Marie Chauvet (SHOW-vay), who had led the friends on their expedition.

Glossary

agriculture the practice of raising plants or animals for human use

anthropology the study of how people have developed and live in cultural groups

archaeologist a scientist who uncovers evidence, or proof, from the past

artifact an object made by people long ago

carbon dating a method of estimating the age of an animal or a plant after it has died

civilization a group of people who have a complex and organized society within a culture

culture the way in which individuals and groups react with their environment, including their technology, customs, beliefs, and art

nomad a person who travels from place to place without a permanent home

prehistory the long period of time before people developed systems of writing and written language

technology the way in which humans produce the items they use